PARTICLE PHYSICS
The New View of the Universe

Christopher F. Lampton

ENSLOW PUBLISHERS, INC.

Bloy St. & Ramsey Ave.
Box 777
Hillside, N.J. 07205
U.S.A.

P.O. Box 38
Aldershot
Hants GU12 6BP
U.K.

Library of Congress Cataloging-In-Publication Data

Lampton, Christopher F.
    Particle physics: the new view of the universe / Christopher Lampton.
        p.   cm.
    Includes index.
    Summary: Discusses our current knowledge of particle physics and the search for the ultimate particle of which everything is made, possibly superstrings.
    ISBN 0-89490-328-4
    1. Particles (Nuclear physics)—Juvenile literature.
    2. Superstring theories—Juvenile literature. 3. Grand unified theories—Juvenile literature. [1. Particles (Nuclear physics) 2. Superstring theories. 3. Grand unified theories (Nuclear physics)] I. Title.

QC793.27.L36   1991

539.7'2—dc20   90-48049
                                                    CIP
                                                    AC
Printed in the United States of America

10 9 8 7 6 5 4 3 2

Illustration Credits:
Dennis Bailey, pp. 13, 14, 17, 23, 25, 31; California Institute of Technology, pp. 22, 53; Fermilab, p. 50; Sheldon H. Glashow, p. 45; NASA, p. 28; National Portrait Gallery, Smithsonian Institute, p. 37; Panasonic, p. 30; Stanford Linear Accelerator Center/U.S. Dept. of Energy, pp. 9, 20, 56; Steven Weinberg, p. 45.

Cover Photo Credit: National Optical Astronomy Observatories.

Contents

1

Simplicity

At some point in your life, you've probably read a mystery novel or at least seen a mystery show on TV. A mystery novel begins with a crime being committed—often a murder. A detective is then called in to find the culprit. As chapter follows chapter, clues to the identity of the criminal are gathered, more crimes are committed, and the plot becomes hopelessly complicated. The reader wonders how the detective will ever make sense of such a disordered jumble of information.

However, in the final chapter, the detective does precisely that. He or she explains that what seemed complicated to the reader is actually quite simple. Underlying all of the crimes and clues is a single criminal (or group of criminals) with a single motive. All of the strange events of the novel occur as a result of that single motive. Everything is neatly tied together and the mystery is brought to a satisfying conclusion.

On the other hand, if the detective were to announce that there was no simple solution to the mystery; that there were, in fact, several completely unrelated criminals at work; that much of what happened in the novel was coincidental or irrelevant . . . well, the reader would most likely hurl the novel across the room in frustration at such an unsatisfactory conclusion. We expect the complex mystery to have a simple explanation (though even simple explanations can sometimes take several pages to set forth).

So it is in the world of science. It is the job of the scientist to gather clues about the nature of the world, then devise simple theories to explain those clues. The simpler the theory and the more clues that it explains, the better the scientist has done his or her work. A scientist is a kind of detective, and the mystery that the scientist is trying to solve is the mystery of the universe!

This description of the scientist's role may seem strange at first encounter. Anyone who has taken a science course knows that scientific theories can be anything but simple; some seem utterly incomprehensible to a struggling student. And every time we pick up a newspaper it seems that some scientist has discovered a fact that makes our world just a little more complicated. So how can we say that scientists are trying to find simple explanations for the mysteries of the universe?

For one thing, this is a description of how science works in a perfect world—but we don't live in a perfect world. The ideal scientific theory would explain everything in the universe in a single sentence or mathematical equation. No such theory has ever been developed, though we shall talk later in this chapter about how scientists are attempting to create just such a theory.

Two Types of Scientists
The second reason has to do with the so-called scientific method. The scientific method breaks the work of scientists into two phases, an experimental phase and a theoretical phase. In the experimental phase, scientists gather as much data as they can about the thing they are studying, usually through carefully planned experiments or through extensive observations. Then, once they have gathered the data, they

devise hypotheses or theories to explain the data. These theories are used to make predictions about the results of further experiments. If these predictions are correct, the theories are accepted. If these predictions are incorrect, the theories are rejected.

It is often the gathering of data in the first phase of the scientific method that makes the world seem so complicated. New facts are discovered through experiment or observation every day. At least once a week, there is a new discovery significant enough to be reported on the front page of the daily newspaper. And all of these discoveries make our view of the universe seem increasingly complex.

What doesn't necessarily get reported on the front page of the newspaper are the theories that scientists devise to explain these discoveries. It is these theories—ideally, at least— that make the world less complicated again.

Because there are two different phases to the scientific method, there tend to be two different types of scientists: experimental scientists and theoretical scientists. Experimental scientists perform the experiments that gather data and verify theories. Theoretical scientists devise the theories that explain the data.

Of course, most scientists have a little of both types in them. No experimental scientist can resist dreaming up theories to explain the data they have gathered. And most theoretical scientists are willing to suggest experiments that might prove or disprove their theories; in fact, this is part of their job. Yet, in practice, most scientists really do think of themselves as being either a theoretical or experimental scientist, even though they may occasionally work on the other side of the fence as well.

Among all the sciences, perhaps the one where the division between experimental science and theoretical science is the sharpest is physics. Physics is the study of the very matter that makes up the universe, and of the forces that act on and within that matter. To many observers, physics is the ultimate science—the one that comes closest to studying the nature of reality itself. And much of the most exciting work being done in science today is being performed within the branch of physics known as "particle physics," which is the study of the tiny particles that make up matter. It is the particle physicists who are on the trail of the "Theory of Everything."

The Theory of Everything

Earlier, we said that the ideal scientific theory would explain the entire universe in a single sentence, or equation. Such a theory might not seem possible—and yet there are scientists who believe that such a "Theory of Everything" is currently within the grasp of physicists. Several years ago, the renowned British physicist Stephen Hawking gave a lecture with the title "Is the End in Sight for Theoretical Physics?" In this lecture, he actually suggested that the basic laws of the universe may soon be known. Physicists may actually be able to describe the universe in a single equation. But what does this really mean? What would such a Theory of Everything actually do? What would it say?

Since the theory is not yet complete—and may, according to some critics, never be complete—it is impossible to know exactly what such a theory would say. Probably it would explain all of the varied phenomena that we see about us—through our eyes, telescopes, and microscopes—in much the same way that a detective solves the mystery in the last chapter of a mystery novel. This theory would show us how everything in the universe fits together—how everything relates to everything else. It would say, in effect, that everything is the way that it is because that is the only way that it could be.

In the four hundred years or so since modern science began, scientists have come a long way. We now know, for instance, that stars shine for the same reason that hydrogen bombs explode, and that planets orbit around stars for the same reason that objects fall to the surface of the earth. We have learned that all of these seemingly unrelated things are related in simple, understandable ways. But this is not enough.

When scientists study the universe they see many things that they can't explain. They don't know why these things are the way that they are. It is as though, at the end of the mystery novel, the detective announced that a certain dead body was dead simply because it was dead, not because somebody had killed it. This would be an unsatisfactory conclusion to a mystery novel. It is an unsatisfactory conclusion to a scientific mystery as well.

Unified Field Theories

The solutions that scientists are now offering for the mysteries of the universe are called unified field theories. These Theories of Everything are an attempt to find the simplest explanations possible for the mysteries of physics. There are many different unified field theories, but none of them is yet complete. At the present time, however, the

Physicists using the "Crystal Ball," a new tool that helps them peer into the atom.

most exciting and promising of these Theories of Everything is called Superstring Theory. It suggests that the universe—stars, planets, galaxies, even space itself—is made up of tiny objects called strings. These strings move, spin, curl up into hoops, and even vibrate like plucked guitar strings. You are made up of these strings, as are all of your friends and neighbors; so is your house, your lawn, the planet earth, and the sun in the sky. (So, in fact, is the sky!)

In the pages that follow, we'll discuss what physicists think they know about the universe right now and what they want to know about it in the future. Most importantly, we'll talk about Superstring Theory, and how it may explain the birth, death, and very existence of the universe itself.

2

Particles

There is no reason that the universe has to be simple. In fact, it may turn out to be a very complicated place indeed. When we read a mystery novel, we know that the solution will turn out to be relatively simple because that's the way mystery novels are usually written. But the universe is not a mystery novel and it does not necessarily follow the same rules.

Yet, when scientists assume that the complicated discoveries they make concerning the universe will turn out to have simple explanations, they are usually correct. When they assume that the universe is more complicated than it seems, they are usually wrong. There is even a name for this principle: *Occam's Razor*. It is named for Sir William of Occam, who said (roughly translated) that the simplest solution that explains all of the facts is usually the best. It is called Occam's Razor because scientists use it to shave away unnecessary complications from their theories.

Most physicists believe deeply in the simplicity of the universe, and this belief has served them well. Perhaps the area where it has served them best is in the search for the ultimate particles of matter.

Atomic Theory

No doubt you have heard of atoms. Everything in the universe—well, almost everything—is made of atoms. (There are objects deep in space that are made out of the same particles that make up atoms, but not out of atoms themselves.) It was only in the last century, though, that this notion was generally accepted by scientists, and only in this century that scientists developed a clear idea of what atoms are like.

When you look at the world around you, you can see that it is made up of a large number of different substances. This book is made of paper. The chair or sofa that you are sitting on is made of wood, metal, or fabric. Your house or apartment is made of bricks and mortar or wood and aluminum.

Thousands of years ago, people had noticed that the world was made up of a large number of different substances. By the beginning of the nineteenth century, literally tens of thousands of different substances were known. A universe constructed of these different substances would seem a complicated place indeed.

But two hundred years ago, scientists noticed that it was possible to take some of these substances apart into other substances, by heating them or subjecting them to various chemicals. It appeared as though some substances were made out of combinations of other substances. There were a few substances, however, that could not be broken down into other substances. Scientists decided that these must be elementary substances, that is, substances that were not made up of other substances. Consequently, these substances came to be called the elements. Substances made up of combinations of various elements were called compounds.

The British chemist John Dalton suggested that elements were made up of tiny particles that he called atoms. This name had first been suggested two thousand years earlier by the ancient Greek philosopher

Democritus. Actually, Democritus called these particles *atomos*, a Greek word meaning "indivisible," because they could not be broken further apart. In a phrase that sounds chillingly modern, Democritus suggested that "in reality, there is nothing but atoms and the void." Alas, this idea fell out of favor in the two millennia following Democritus' time. Then, Dalton's atomic theory caught on, and for the remainder of the nineteenth century, most scientists agreed that matter was made up of atoms—even if they had no idea of what these atoms were like.

The remarkable thing about atomic theory was that it reduced the tens of thousands of substances that had previously been believed to make up the world to only a few dozen atoms. This was a wonderful simplification, a vindication of the scientists' belief that a great

Democritus, the ancient philosopher who first came up with the idea of the atom, an ultimate particle of which all things are made. He believed, wrongly, that this particle was indivisible (*atomos* in Greek).

simplicity underlies the seeming complexity of the universe. But greater simplification lay ahead.

Inside the Atom

In the early years of the twentieth century, physicists discovered that the atom was not, in fact, indivisible, as both Dalton and Democritus had believed. Matter was made up of atoms, true, but the atoms themselves were constructed of particles called the electron, proton, and neutron. It's traditional to imagine the atom as a kind of miniature solar system, with the protons and neutrons clustered in the center as a kind of "sun" and the electrons whizzing around it in orbits like tiny planets. (That's not really what the atom is like, but it's easier to visualize this way; the real structure of the atom is very hard to picture.) The number of protons in an atom determines of what element

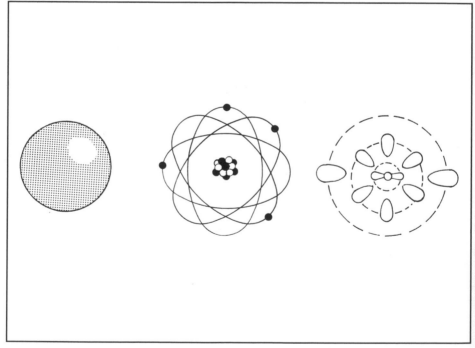

Three concepts of the atom: (from left to right) a. Democritus's vision of a solid particle; b. the atom made up of protons and neutrons and electrons with regular orbits; c. the quantum view of the atom.

it is an atom. The numbers of neutrons and electrons have subtler effects on the way in which it interacts with other atoms.

From this new picture of the atom emerged a new branch of physics called quantum theory. We don't have room in this book to discuss the full length and breadth of quantum theory, but many of the ideas discussed in this and later chapters are part of the theory. The basis behind quantum theory is the idea that events in the world of the very small, the world of subatomic particles, are not deterministic. This means that effects do not follow causes in the way that we believe they do in the larger world of which we are a part. You cannot make absolute predictions about events in the quantum world. You can only give the probability that an event will take place, much as weather forecasters give the probability that it will rain or snow. Not surprisingly, quantum theory revolutionized the way that physicists and other scientists looked at the universe.

Perhaps the most important thing about the revolutionary new theories that dominated physics in the early twentieth century is the way in which they simplified our view of the universe. Not only could the thousands of different substances known to science be reduced to a few dozen atoms, but now the few dozen atoms could, in turn, be reduced to a mere three particles. All matter in the universe, or so it seemed by the 1930s, was made up of a mere three particles. This was a major triumph for the theoretical physicists and their belief in the underlying simplicity of the universe.

Then the experimental physicists stepped in and started making things more complicated again. Before we tell you what they discovered, however, let's pause for a brief look at the methods physicists use to study the ultimate nature of matter.

Seeing the Unseeable

How do you "see" something that is too far away or too small for the human eye to detect? This is a problem with which science has wrestled for hundreds of years, and for which some ingenious solutions have been designed. One of these solutions is the telescope, which draws in large quantities of light from distant stars and galaxies, allowing astronomers to see distant objects that would otherwise go unnoticed. Another solution is the microscope, which magnifies the images of tiny objects, allowing biologists and chemists to see things too small for the naked eye to see otherwise.

But neither the telescope nor the microscope can help the particle physicist explore the world of the very small particles that make up matter. It is important to understand why this is so.

When you look at the world around you, you see one thing and only one thing: light. Although you may think that you are seeing books, people, buildings, clouds and other things, you are actually seeing light that has bounced off of these things and entered your eyes. Your eyes contain special receptors for detecting this light and analyzing the information that it contains about the objects off which it has bounced. Your brain then uses this information to create a three-dimensional picture of the world around you. So smoothly and seemingly effortlessly does your brain perform this job that you are not even aware that all you are seeing is light (unless you stare directly into a light bulb, of course).

Just as matter is made up of particles called atoms (which in turn are made up of smaller particles called electrons, neutrons, and protons), so light is made up of smaller particles called photons. It is these particles that bounce off of the objects around you and enter your eyes, allowing you to see those objects. In effect, these particles are "messengers," carrying information about the world to your eyes.

As long as the objects we are looking at are relatively large, this is an excellent way of receiving information about them. However, it is not such a good way to receive information about smaller objects.

For example, imagine that you are in a completely dark room, unable to receive information about your surroundings through light. Instead, you must "see" by throwing a rubber ball and determining whether or not it bounces back at you. If you throw a rubber ball at a wall, for instance, it will bounce straight back at you. You will then know that there is a large solid object directly in front of you. But if you throw the rubber ball at a smaller object than a wall, such as a basketball, table lamp, or even another rubber ball, it will not bounce back at you. It will simply knock the object aside and keep on going. Not only will you not be able to "see" the object, but you will actually change its position. You will alter the world around you by the very act of observing it.

Something similar happens when scientists try to investigate the world of the very small, the world of atoms. They cannot "see" such particles using ordinary light, because the photons of light are simply too large. When a photon hits an electron or a proton, it doesn't bounce off, it knocks the particle aside. Thus, an ordinary light microscope is

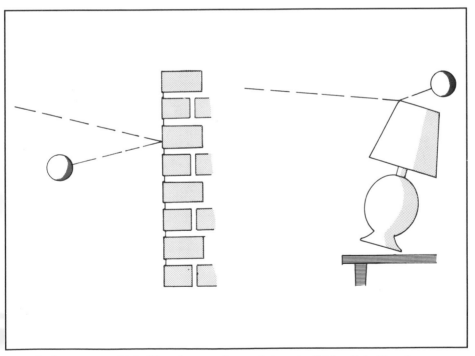

In the same way this ball knocks over a lamp, photons (or light particles) knock over tiny particles like electrons, making it impossible to see them.

useless for looking at things this small. We need smaller particles to bounce off of these small things.

A special type of microscope called an electron microscope uses electrons rather than photons to look at very small objects. But even an electron microscope is useless for viewing anything smaller than a very large atom. To look at the particles studied by particle physicists, we need a way to see even smaller details.

Particle or Wave?
There is a problem with using very small particles to "see" other particles. Early in this century, it was learned that the particles that make up matter are not like particles of dust, or sand, or tiny little billiard balls. In fact, they are not precisely like anything that we encounter in everyday life. What makes these particles strange is that they are as much like waves—water waves, say, or sound waves—as they are like particles.

How can a particle be like a wave? That's a difficult question to answer because the waves we are discussing here are not exactly like waves of water or waves of sound. They are what physicists refer to as probability waves, a kind of wave that is difficult to picture because it is like nothing in our ordinary experience. Suffice it to say that physicists know that these particles are like waves because their wave nature has been demonstrated in experiment after experiment. For the time being you will simply have to accept that this is the way things are in the world of subatomic particles.

Not only do the particles that make up matter have both a wave nature and a particle nature, but so does everything else in the universe (because everything else is made up of these particles). You have a wave nature, as does this book, your house, the planet earth, etc. But in a very large object, such as you or this book, the wave nature is quite unnoticeable—even undetectable. With an object smaller than an atom, on the other hand, the wave nature becomes dominant and the particle nature is pushed into the background. Thus, when we speak

of things that small, we are speaking of things that are much more like waves than like particles. And when we use particles that small to "see" by, we are bouncing waves off of other waves as much as we are bouncing particles off of other particles.

This isn't necessarily bad. In theory, we can see as readily with waves as with particles. But using smaller and smaller particles to see by doesn't mean that we will be using smaller and smaller waves. In particles this small it is the wavelength that determines what we can see, not the size of the particle itself. The shorter the wavelength, the smaller the details we can discern with our "microscope."

Fortunately, there is a way to make the wavelength of a particle shorter. We can give a particle additional energy, which in practice means we accelerate it to extremely high speeds. The faster a particle moves, the shorter its wavelength becomes, and the smaller the things we can see with the aid of that particle. A microscope for particle physicists, then, would use fast moving particles.

Cosmic Rays and Particle Accelerators

Is it possible to build such a microscope? Yes, and in fact, physicists in the 1940s discovered that such a microscope already exists in nature. It's called a cosmic ray shower.

Cosmic rays come shooting into the earth's atmosphere from somewhere in distant space. They may be created in ferocious explosions in some distant part of our galaxy. Every now and then one of these particles plunges into the earth's atmosphere, like an extremely tiny meteorite. Within a fraction of a second, it collides with one of the particles that make up the earth's atmosphere.

Because the particle from space is moving at tremendous speeds (often very close to the speed of light), the resulting collision involves tremendous amounts of energy. The energy from the collision has to go somewhere, so it is turned into still more particles.

The great German-American physicist Albert Einstein, in his Special Theory of Relativity, revealed that matter and energy are interchangeable—that they are, in fact, two forms of the same thing. Under the right conditions, matter can turn into energy and energy into matter. And this is precisely what happens when the cosmic ray particle collides with a particle of the earth's atmosphere. The energy of the cosmic ray's motion through space is converted into a shower of brand-new particles, freshly formed out of pure energy.

Not all of the energy of the original particle is converted into new particles. Some of it is still around in the form of energy, so these new particles are moving quite rapidly themselves. They, in turn, collide with still other particles of the atmosphere, and still more particles are formed. The result is a cosmic ray shower, a cascade of energetic particles raining down from the sky.

In the late 1940s, physicists began observing cosmic ray showers by placing boxes filled with layers of photographic plates high up on

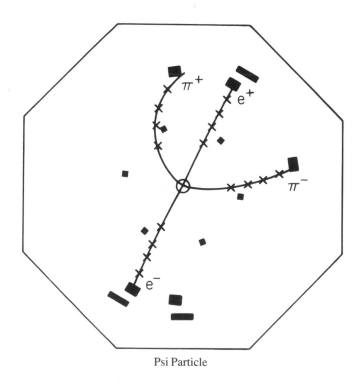

Psi Particle

mountaintops. When a cosmic ray shower occurred, the particles in the shower left marks on the plates, which were clearly visible when the plates were developed. By studying the marks on the plates, physicists learned much about the way these particles moved and interacted with each other—which, in turn, told them a great deal about the particles themselves.

Soon after these cosmic ray experiments began, physicists developed their own "microscopes" for viewing extremely small particles. These new devices were called particle accelerators. They used giant magnets for accelerating particles to extremely high speeds, then colliding them with one another. These collisions produce new particles in the same way that cosmic ray collisions produced new particles. In addition, the way in which the particles "bounce" after the collisions tells physicists much about the particles themselves, the same way that bouncing photons tell our eyes and brain about the world around us.

Not all of the particles observed in cosmic ray showers and in particle accelerators were electrons, protons, and neutrons. Many new particles were discovered—much to the surprise of physicists who had believed that the secrets of matter had already been uncovered. In fact, by the 1960s literally hundreds of new particles had been discovered. Almost all of these particles were of a type known to physicists as hadrons. Two kinds of hadrons, the protons and neutrons, were already known before these experiments were performed, but many new and previously unknown types of hadrons were discovered.

Particle accelerators are still the most important tool that physicists possess for studying the ultimate nature of the world around us. Every few years a larger, more powerful accelerator is built. The larger the accelerator, the more energy can be put into the speeding particles. This shortens the wavelength of the particles, allowing smaller and smaller details to be examined when particles collide. In addition, the greater energy allows heavier particles to be created out of the energy of the collisions.

Particles Inside Particles

The baffling array of hadrons discovered in cosmic ray showers and particle accelerators presented physicists with a new problem: how to find order in the midst of such chaos. Just as the physicists of the early nineteenth century had been forced to come to terms with the multitude of substances that they saw in the world around them, so the physicists of the 1960s were forced to sort out the multitude of particles they had discovered and make some sense of them. The nineteenth-century physicists had solved their problem by invoking atomic theory and reducing tens of thousands of compounds to a few dozen elements. Could the twentieth-century physicists do something similar to reduce the number of hadrons?

Yes, and in the early 1960s the American physicists Murray Gell-Mann and George Zweig independently suggested that most of these new particles were no more "elementary" than was the atom. Rather, just as an atom is made up of electrons, protons, and neutrons, so the hadrons were made up of still smaller particles. Gell-Mann called these particles quarks, after a nonsense word in James Joyce's

Dr. Murray Gell-Mann, discoverer of the quark.

novel *Finnegan's Wake*. (Zweig called them aces, but the name did not catch on.)

According to Gell-Mann, each hadron is made up of three quarks. Quarks themselves come in several different flavors, which we now call up, down, strange, charm, top, and bottom. (The latter two flavors are also sometimes called truth and beauty.) In addition, each flavor of quark comes in three colors, often referred to as red, yellow and blue. (The quarks are not really colored, in the sense that objects in the world around you are colored; rather, scientists use the word "color" to describe something more abstract about the quarks that cannot be seen.)

With this one ingenious theory, Gell-Mann reduced the hundreds of known hadrons to just six different quarks (eighteen, if we count all three colors of each flavor). Every hadron is made from a different

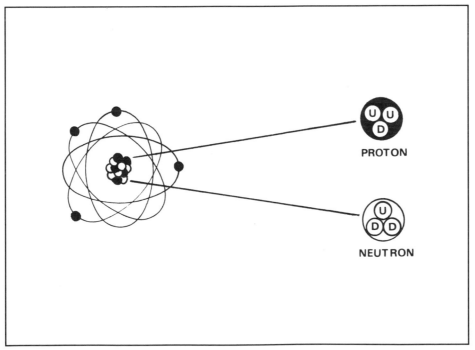

Both protons and neutrons are made of quarks. Protons consist of two up quarks and one down quark, while neutrons consist of two down quarks and one up quark.

combination of these quarks. The neutron, for instance, is made up of one up quark and two down quarks. The proton is made up of two up quarks and one down quark.

In addition to the six quarks, physicists know of six more elementary particles of matter. They are the electron, electron neutrino, muon, muon neutrino, tau particle and tau neutrino. These six particles are known collectively as the leptons.

The difference between these particles lies in the type of forces that can act on them. This and other properties are described by their so-called quantum numbers. These are the identifying numbers that physicists use to describe a particle, and they are determined through experiment. Quantum numbers describe such properties of the particle as mass (a property that determines the particle's weight), charge, spin, parity, strangeness, charm, color, etc. We'll be talking further about some of these quantum numbers and what they mean in the next chapter.

In addition to the six quarks and six leptons just mentioned, there are also six anti-quarks and six anti-leptons. These are particles that are identical to the ordinary quarks and leptons in every way except that all the quantum numbers (except mass and spin) are reversed. Collectively, these anti-particles are known as antimatter. When a particle collides with its anti-particle, it is possible for the two to convert into pure radiation. This is the reverse of the process by which energy is converted into matter.

The six leptons, six quarks, and their twelve anti-particles make up all matter that we know about. (There are also several particles, including the photon, that transmit forces between other particles, which we'll talk more about in the next chapter.)

Yet even this collection of twelve particles is considered too complex by many physicists. For one thing, most matter in the universe (as far as we know, anyway) is made up of only three of these particles—the up quark, the down quark, and the electron. The other nine particles (and their antiparticles) seem largely irrelevant and physicists are not quite sure why they exist.

You might argue, of course, that particles don't need a reason to exist in order to exist. This may be true, but these seemingly irrelevant particles still offend those physicists who believe in the underlying simplicity of nature. Later, we'll see how Superstring Theory offers the possibility of the ultimate simplification in particle theory.

The twenty-four particles named in the preceding paragraphs are not all of the particles that physicists know about. The particles discussed in this chapter are the particles of matter, but there is a second kind of particle in the universe as well. We've already met one of these non-matter particles: the photon. In the next chapter, we'll meet several more.

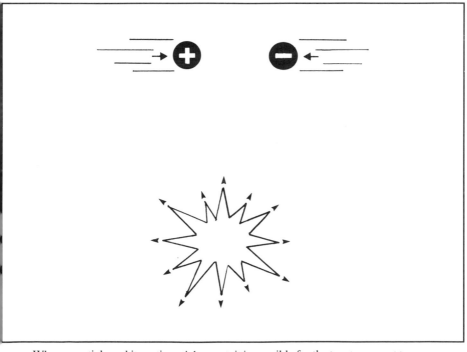

When a particle and its anti-particle meet, it is possible for the two to convert to pure radiation.

3
Interactions

Without matter particles, the universe would be very different. Planets, stars and human beings—to name but three things that are made up of matter—would not exist. The universe would be a dull place indeed.

But, as it turns out, you can't have a universe made up of nothing but matter particles. There must be a way for matter particles to interact with each other. Otherwise, the universe would be a thin soup of particles that would never stick together long enough to form stars, planets, and so forth. And, in fact, there is a second class of particle that is responsible for interactions between matter particles.

What do we mean by the word "interactions"? When one thing influences another thing—that is, when the first thing causes the second thing to change in some way—we say that they have interacted. When you bump into a person in the hallway, for instance, the two of you have interacted: you have changed the other person's motion in the hallway and the other person has changed yours. You can also interact with a person simply by talking to them or even by letting them look at you. In each case, the other person will be changed in some way by the interaction, if only by having an image of you impressed on his or her brain cells. Doubtless you will be changed in some way by the interaction too.

Two particles are said to interact when they cause each other to change in some way. Often the change is a change in motion: two particles may attract or repel one another, and thus, change their direction of motion. In other cases, two particles can interact in such a way that their quantum numbers change—the interacting particles actually change into different types of particles.

It is traditional to say that these interactions are caused by forces, as though something had actually reached across the space between the particles and "forced" them to change. However, the word *force* can be misleading; the word *interaction* better describes what takes place between the particles. In this book, we will use the words force and interaction interchangeably. In particle physics, they mean almost the same thing.

Physicists are currently aware of four interactions that take place between particles. They are the strong interaction, weak interaction, electromagnetic interaction and gravitational interaction. Alternatively, we can refer to them as the strong force, weak force, electromagnetic force, and gravitational force. (The strong and weak forces are sometimes referred to as the strong and weak nuclear forces.)

The Gravitational Interaction

The most familiar of these interactions is the gravitational interaction. It is the gravitational interaction that is pulling you down into your chair even as you read this book. More specifically, it is the gravitational interaction between the particles that make up your body and the particles that make up the planet earth that is pulling you down.

The strength of the gravitational interaction between two particles is determined by the property called mass. The larger the mass is for a given particle, the more strongly it interacts through gravity with other particles. The electron has a very small mass, so electrons do not have a very strong gravitational interaction with other particles. The proton and neutron, on the other hand, have relatively large masses. Thus, they have a stronger gravitational interaction with other particles than the electron does.

Most of the mass of your body, for instance, is in the protons and neutrons that it contains. This is why mass is intimately connected with the concept of weight. The greater the collective mass of all of the particles in our bodies, the greater the effect that the earth's gravity

Neptune and its moon Triton. Gravitational interaction keeps moons and other satellites from flying out of orbit around their host planets.

has on us—and the more we weigh. Of course, if we were to travel deep into outer space, we would no longer have weight because there would be no large collections of particles nearby, such as the earth, to interact with us gravitationally. But we would still have mass and would still interact gravitationally with any large bodies that we might approach.

The gravitational interaction is far and away the weakest of the four interactions, even though it is the one that has the most obvious effect on our daily lives. (The electromagnetic force also has a profound effect on our daily lives, though this effect is not obvious until it is pointed out—as we will do in the next section.) The weak interaction (which, despite its name, is not the weakest interaction) is vastly more powerful than the gravitational interaction. The electromagnetic interaction and the strong interaction are stronger still.

You might wonder why the gravitational interaction seems so strong to human beings while the other, stronger interactions seem so negligible. The answer is that we are experiencing the cumulative gravitational interaction of an incredibly large number of particles—the particles that make up our bodies, the earth, sun, and so on—which has the effect of multiplying the minuscule gravitational interactions of the individual particles. For various reasons, the other interactions do not have such a cumulative effect.

The Electromagnetic Interaction

The second most familiar of the interactions is the electromagnetic interaction. As its name implies, it is the interaction that is responsible for magnets and electricity. Less obviously, it is also responsible for radio, TV, and the very light that we see by. In addition, it is the electromagnetic force that holds small masses of matter, such as TV sets and dogs, together. (Thus, the effect of the electromagnetic force on our daily lives is at least as profound as that of gravity—if not more so.)

Just as the quantum number known as mass determines the

gravitational interaction between two particles, so the electromagnetic interaction is determined by the quantum number known as electric charge. The charge of a particle can be zero (in which case it does not take part in the electromagnetic interaction), or it can be some multiple of -1 or +1 (in which case it does take part in the electromagnetic interaction). The charge of an electron, for instance, is -1. The charge of the proton is +1.

If the signs on the charges of two particles (that is, + or -) are the same, we say that they have like charges. Particles with like charges—a pair of protons, for instance—repel one another electromagnetically. If the signs on the charges of two particles are different, we say that they have opposite charges. Particles with opposite charges—an electron and a proton, for instance—attract one another.

The Strong Interaction

The strong interaction is the strongest of all the known interactions. It acts on the particles that we call hadrons. In fact, the original definition

Electromagnetic interaction makes it possible for this radio to work.

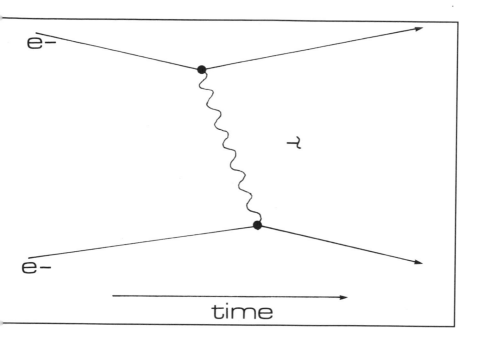

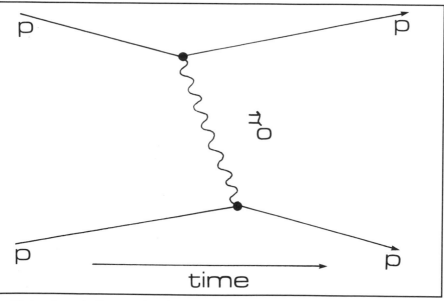

These schematic diagrams show how physicists view the electromagnetic interaction (above) and the strong interaction (below).

of a hadron was "a particle that takes part in the strong interaction." (Now we define hadrons as particles that are made up of quarks, a point on which we will elaborate in a moment.) Unlike the electromagnetic interaction, the strong interaction between hadrons is always attractive; that is, a pair of hadrons will always attract and never repel one another. Protons and neutrons attract one another, as do neutrons and other neutrons and protons and other protons. For that matter, any hadron will attract any other hadron.

It is the combination of the electromagnetic and nuclear forces that holds an atom together. The electromagnetic interaction between the protons in the nucleus and the electrons orbiting the nucleus is what keeps the electrons from flying out of the atom. (Nonetheless, there are circumstances under which the electrons in orbit about the nucleus can be torn loose from the atom.) The strong interaction between the hadrons in the nucleus is what holds the nucleus together. The fact that the strong interaction is substantially stronger than the electromagnetic interaction is important here, since the electromagnetic repulsion between the protons in the nucleus would tear the nucleus apart if their strong attraction were not greater still.

The Weak Interaction
The weak interaction is the least well-known of the four interactions. It is the weak interaction that best justifies the use of the word *interaction* rather than the word *force*, because it does not behave in the manner we normally associate with forces. The weak interaction actually changes the quantum numbers associated with two particles in such a way that the particles become different particles.

As far as we know, everything that happens in the universe around us happens as a result of one or several of these four interactions. Atoms, for instance, are held together to form larger chunks of matter by the electromagnetic force; thus, without the electromagnetic interaction, there would be no books, houses, cars, or human beings. The nuclear reactions that power the sun and other stars are mostly caused by a combination of the weak and strong interactions. Though the other interactions also play a role, very large chunks of matter, such as the earth and sun, are held together primarily by the gravitational interaction, as are solar systems, galaxies, clusters of galaxies, and so on.

So important are these interactions that particle physicists have spent much of their time and effort working out the precise rules by which these interactions take place. Some of what they have discovered has been surprising indeed.

Messenger Particles

Perhaps the most surprising discovery, to which we alluded at the beginning of this chapter, is that these interactions are mediated, or carried, by particles. In fact, there is a class of particles that are responsible for making these interactions take place.

The particles that we described in the last chapter are particles of matter. Physicists have a special name for these matter particles. They call them fermions, after the Italian-American physicist Enrico Fermi who first described the way in which they behave. But not all particles in the universe are fermions. There is a second class of particles that physicists refer to as bosons, after the Indian physicist Satyendra Bose who first described the way in which these particles behave. Bosons are the particles responsible for interactions among other particles.

Specifically, the interactions are carried by virtual bosons, particles that flicker in and out of existence so mysteriously that they cannot be detected in a physicist's laboratory, except by the forces that they carry between particles. Oddly, the amount of time that such a virtual particle may remain in existence is determined by its mass—the more massive the particle, the shorter its life span. We'll see in a moment why this is important.

In the 1930s, the Japanese physicist Hideki Yukawa suggested that the strong force might be carried between hadrons by virtual bosons that he called mesons. This idea solved a couple of problems at a single stroke. One of these was the problem of "force at a distance."

Physicists have never much cared for the idea of non-local interactions, that is, the notion that something in one place could interact with something in another place without first crossing the distance between them. Yet the forces or interactions known to physicists seemed to do just that. Particles are not in physical contact with one another when they interact, and yet, they nonetheless affect one another. How are they able to do this?

Yukawa suggested that when two particles interacted, they were actually exchanging virtual "messenger" particles. In effect, one particle emits a virtual particle and sends it to the other particle as a way of saying "I am interacting with you." The other particle sends a virtual particle back to the first particle saying "I am interacting with you, too."

As odd as this notion may seem on the face of it, it also explains another important aspect of particle interactions: why different interactions have different ranges. The gravitational and electromagnetic interactions, for instance, can function over infinite distances (though they grow weaker with distance), while the weak and strong forces only work over extremely short distances—typical of the distances between particles in an atomic nucleus. Yukawa suggested that this was a result of the masses of the virtual particles that carried these interactions. We saw a moment ago that the lifespan of a virtual particle is determined by its mass. The virtual particles that mediated the gravitational and electromagnetic interactions must be massless because they have unlimited lifetimes, and therefore, can work over infinite distances. The strong and weak forces, on the other hand, must be mediated by relatively massive particles, which can only exist for a very short period of time before they must wink out of existence again. Thus, they can only travel tiny distances.

Yukawa used this theory to calculate what the meson, which he believed to be the carrier of the strong force, must be like. And when the meson was later discovered in particle accelerator experiments, he turned out to be correct.

If the meson is the carrier of the strong force, what are the carriers of the other forces? Surprisingly, the electromagnetic force is carried by virtual photons, the particles of light. The weak force is carried by the so-called W and Z particles. And gravity is carried by a particle named the graviton. The graviton, however, has not yet been detected experimentally. In fact, it interacts so weakly with other particles that it may never be detected.

All of these messenger particles are bosons. Although the bosons that carry the interactions between particles are virtual bosons, there are also real bosons, as you can see every time you open your eyes: the photons of everyday light are very real, not virtual at all, which is why your eyes are able to detect them. Just as many physicists consider the number of known matter particles to be excessive, they also feel that there are too many bosons—and too many interactions. It would greatly simplify our view of the universe if there were only one type of boson and one type of interaction. Things would be even simpler if there were only one type of particle . . . period. In the next two chapters, we'll see how physicists are seriously considering this possibility. And in the last chapter, we'll see how superstring theory may make this vision of a grand unification of all interactions and particles come true!

4

Unification

The dawn of the twentieth century saw a great revolution in physics. In fact, it saw two revolutions, and their names were quantum theory and relativity. So far in this book, we've been discussing quantum theory. Now let's talk for a moment about relativity.

Relativity
Relativity is actually two related theories, both created by the great physicist Albert Einstein in the early years of the twentieth century. In the first of these, called the Special Theory of Relativity, Einstein proposed (among other things) the idea that matter and energy are interchangeable, that one can be converted into the other. In the second, the General Theory of Relativity, Einstein tackled a subject that most physicists believed was already completely understood: the nature of the gravitational interaction.

Like Yukawa in the 1930s, Einstein was troubled by the notion of force at a distance. In the traditional gravitational theory of Newton, the gravitational interaction moved instantaneously across space, traveling infinite distances in no time at all.

This troubled Einstein because he knew that nothing could move instantaneously across space. In fact, as he himself had shown in the Special Theory of Relativity, nothing could move faster than the speed of light, which is 186,000 miles (300,000 kilometers) per second. Thus, this was the maximum speed at which the gravitational interaction (or any other force) could move across space.

But what was the gravitational interaction? How could it travel through the intervening space between two particles? What was actually doing the traveling?

Einstein decided that gravitation could be understood as arising from the curvature of space and time. A massive particle, or collection of particles, actually bends space in a way that affects the motion of

Albert Einstein (1879-1955), thought by many to be the greatest physicist of the twentieth century. His Special Theory of Relativity is the ground work for today's research.

other particles. Those particles then move toward it, as though they were attracted by a force. The more massive the collection of particles, the more profoundly did it bend space, and the more dramatically were other collections of particles attracted toward it. Hence, planets and suns produced more gravity than books, human beings, or individual particles.

Although this was certainly a radical notion in its time—and, in fact, still sounds rather radical today—it was soon verified by experiment.

Dueling Metaphors

But wait a minute! Didn't we say in the last chapter that the gravitational interaction was carried by a messenger particle called the graviton? Yes, we did. Yet now we're saying that gravity is a curve in space. Which of these descriptions is true?

Alas, they both are, which has become the source of much confusion—even among scientists. In a sense, we can consider the relativistic description of gravity as a curving of space and the quantum description of gravity as an exchange of virtual gravitons as metaphors, symbolic descriptions of a process that cannot be described in normal words. This doesn't disturb physicists too much, because they usually prefer not to describe such things in words at all. They prefer to describe them using mathematics, the language of numbers. Quite often, different metaphors for a physical process will produce the same mathematical descriptions, so that physicists are not troubled by what seem to the rest of us to be contradictions.

Unfortunately, there are contradictions between the relativistic view of gravity and the quantum view of gravity—even when expressed mathematically. And therein lies one of the great problems of modern physics: how to unify the relativistic description of gravity with the quantum description of the other three interactions.

Quantum Electrodynamics

But before we talk further about the unification of relativity and quantum theory, let's talk a little more about the quantum theories that have been devised to explain electromagnetism, the strong interaction and the weak interaction. In particular, let's talk about QED.

QED stands for quantum electrodynamics. It is the theory that describes the workings of the electromagnetic interaction. It is regarded by physicists as the most successful scientific theory of all time, because it makes the most accurate predictions of any theory. In fact, the predictions made by QED have become legendary among physicists.

QED was not an easy theory to develop. The search for a comprehensive quantum description of the electromagnetic interaction began in the early 1930s and lasted for nearly two decades. The main problem in developing the theory was the problem of the infinities. Whenever physicists tried to calculate certain numbers concerning the electromagnetic interaction, such as the strength of the electromagnetic interaction, they kept coming up with infinite values, and this clearly made no sense.

To get an idea why these infinite values kept cropping up, let's talk about the inverse square principle. Whenever you have a "force" that radiates outward in all directions from a source, such as a particle, you'll find that the force grows weaker with distance according to very strict rules. Specifically, it grows weaker at the inverse square of the distance.

How's that again? If you've taken mathematics courses, you're probably aware that a square is a number multiplied times itself. The square of 2 is 4, the square of 3 is 9, the square of 4 is 16, and so forth. The inverse of a number is simply the number turned upside down. The inverse of 1/2 is 2/1 (or just 2), the inverse of 3/4 is 4/3, the inverse of 9 is 1/9, and so on. An inverse square, then, is a number multiplied times itself, then turned upside down. The inverse square of 2 is 1/4, the inverse square of 3 is 1/9, the inverse square of 4 is 1/16, and so forth.

What does that have to do with the strength of a force or interaction? Suppose that we measure the strength of a force at a certain distance from its source. If we then move twice as far away, we'll find that the force is only 1/4 as strong. If we move three times as far away, the force will be only 1/9 as strong. If we move four times as far away, the force will be only 1/16 as strong, and so forth. In other words, the strength of the force is falling off at the inverse square of the distance.

What happens if, instead of moving away from the force, we move toward it? The same thing happens, only in reverse. At 1/2 the distance, the force will be 4 times as strong. At 1/3 the distance, the force will be 9 times as strong. At 1/4 the distance, the force will be 16 times as strong, and so forth.

This concept isn't hard to understand. Indeed, scientists have known about and understood the inverse square principle since the time of Sir Isaac Newton. But the inverse square principle does leave some unanswered questions, which become important when calculating the strength of forces produced by particles that are infinitesimally small.

One obvious question may have occurred to you when you were reading the description of the inverse square principle in the preceding paragraphs: What will happen when you actually arrive at the source of the force? How strong will the force be when you are in physical contact with the object or particle that is producing it? At that point, you can no longer say that you are so many times a certain distance from the source of the force because you will actually be there. You will be no distance at all from the source of the force.

Surprisingly, this situation usually doesn't come up—not in everyday life, at least. Consider, for instance, the gravitational force produced by the planet earth. Even as you read this book, you are in physical contact with the earth, or at least in contact with an object such as a floor that is, in turn, in contact with the earth. And the gravitational force of the earth doesn't feel much different than it does when you are on, say, the one-hundredth floor of a skyscraper or flying in an airplane.

But, the truth is, you are not really in contact with the source of the earth's gravitational attraction at all. Rather, you are in contact with a few of the many, many particles that together produce the earth's gravity. You can never be in physical contact with all of them at the same time, so you can never actually "arrive" at the source of this gravitational force.

This may seem like a silly point, but really it isn't. According to the equations worked out by Newton, the earth's gravitation appears to us to be emanating from the very center of the earth, which is 4,000 miles (6,440 kilometers) below your feet. So you are actually still 4,000 miles from the source of this particular force. You have not yet arrived.

Can we, then, move closer to the source of the earth's gravity by digging a hole and burrowing toward the center of the earth? No, because we would then place a certain amount of the earth's mass— that is, a certain number of the particles that produce the earth's gravity—above us, where it would cancel out the gravitational attraction of the mass below us. Thus, the intensity of the earth's gravity would actually seem to diminish as we approached the center of the earth, effectively becoming zero at the center itself. The truth is, we are as close to the source of the earth's gravity here at the surface as we can ever be—and, yet, that source is still four thousand miles away. There is no way to test the question of what the inverse square law means when we actually arrive at the source.

The situation is different when we are calculating the intensity of the electromagnetic interaction produced by an electron. According to most physicists, the electron is a point particle, as are all truly elementary particles. This means that the electron has no size at all, but is only a geometric point. It is, therefore, possible for two particles—an electron, say, and a proton—to come infinitely close to one another. It is possible, in effect, to arrive at the source of the force.

And what happens then? According to the traditional mathematical interpretation of the inverse square law, the force becomes stronger without limit; it becomes infinitely strong. What does that mean? How can anything have infinite strength? Is such a thing even possible?

According to physicists, it is not. The concept of infinite strength has no meaning. And for a while it began to look as though the inverse square law, one of the most cherished principles of physics, might be incorrect.

Renormalization

This was the situation faced by the physicists of the 1930s. They were stymied by the concept of infinite strength, which was considered one of the great problems of physics, one which needed to be worked out before quantum theory could provide a coherent picture of the universe.

Werner Heisenberg, the great German physicist who discovered the uncertainty principle, proposed an ingenious solution to the problem. Heisenberg suggested that space was discontinuous, that it had a grainy quality to it. We might compare this idea of discontinuous space to the way in which pictures are printed in a newspaper or book. If you look closely at a printed picture, you will see that it is actually made up of a network of dots, called half-tone dots. Similarly, the picture on a computer video display is made up of dots called pixels (short for "pictorial elements"). No amount of detail smaller than a pixel—half a pixel, say, or two-thirds of a pixel—can be displayed on a computer screen.

In effect, Heisenberg was saying that the universe broke down into pixels, and no smaller amount of detail was possible. The pixels of the universe are so small that we cannot detect them, which is why we believe that space is smooth and continuous, when actually it is not.

This meant that there actually is a limit to how closely two particles could approach one another. They can occupy adjacent "pixels," but they can come no closer than that. Thus, the problem of infinite closeness, and therefore, infinite force, never arises.

Heisenberg's proposal was largely ignored, and is today nearly forgotten. In the 1940s, physicists chose a different method for resolving the problem of the infinities. That method, which was used by the scientists developing QED, is called renormalization.

The idea behind renormalization is difficult and we won't be discussing it in much detail here. Basically, it is a way of getting rid of infinities by finding more infinities and allowing them to cancel each other out, the way you cancel numbers on the opposite sides of the equals sign when solving an equation in algebra class.

When this idea was first proposed in the late 1940s, many physicists felt that it was a cheap mathematical trick, a phony way of playing one infinity off of another.

But the theory worked. When QED was used to predict the strength of the electromagnetic interaction in various situations, its predictions were startlingly accurate, more accurate than the predictions of any theory before or since—on any subject whatsoever. Although renormalization might seem like a cheap mathematical trick, the success of the theory led otherwise dubious physicists to accept it anyway.

Quantum Chromodynamics

When physicists began working out a theory of the strong interaction in the 1960s, they modeled it after QED, even going so far as to name it quantum chromodynamics, or QCD. The "chromo" in the name comes from the fact that the strong interaction between hadrons turned out to be a mere vestige of an even stronger interaction called the color force that acted between quarks. Just as atoms in molecules (chains of atoms) are held together by the same electromagnetic force that holds electrons in orbit about the nucleus of the atom, so hadrons within the atomic nucleus are held together by the same color force that binds the quarks inside the hadrons themselves. This force is carried by a type of boson known as the gluon.

The reason that the full strength of the color force is never seen in the laboratory is that quarks themselves are never seen outside of hadrons. And the reason that quarks are never seen outside of hadrons was one of the great revelations of QCD.

Unlike other interactions, which grow stronger as the interacting particles grow closer to one another, the color force actually grows stronger as the quarks move apart from one another. This phenomenon is known as asymptotic freedom. As long as they are bound together inside hadrons, quarks can move about freely, having little effect on one another. But if they try to break out of their "cell," the color interaction between the quarks grows more intense, as though they were held together by a rubber band that binds them more tightly as they grow farther apart. If a quark gains enough energy to snap the rubber band, that energy is then converted into new quarks, which bind with the escaping quarks to form new hadrons. Thus, free quarks are never seen.

Like QED, quantum chromodynamics suffers from a plague of pesky infinities; and, like QED, it is renormalizable. That is, the infinities can be used to cancel one another out. However, the experimental predictions produced by QCD are not quite as accurate as those produced by the phenomenally successful QED. Still, QCD is accurate enough to be considered a successful theory.

These two theories, QED and QCD, give us the best descriptions that we have of the way in which the electromagnetic and strong interactions behave. But what about the other two interactions, the weak interaction and gravity? What theories have been worked out to explain their behavior in quantum terms?

Electroweak Theory
At first, when scientists approached the problem in the 1950s and 1960s, it seemed as though the weak interaction would not yield to the same sort of theoretical scrutiny as the electromagnetic and strong interactions. Then, three physicists named Sheldon Glashow, Stephen Weinberg and Abdus Salam made independent contributions to an

inspired idea. What if the weak interaction was actually just another form of the electromagnetic interaction?

You would think that if this were so—if electromagnetism and the weak interaction were two different parts of a single interaction—that physicists would have noticed this fact a long time ago. But that isn't necessarily true. What Glashow, Weinberg, and Salam suggested was that the two interactions had once been a single interaction, but that something had happened subsequently to make them look different. And that is why physicists had never noticed that they were actually the same.

What could make two interactions "look" different? When our universe was born, between fifteen and twenty billion years ago, it was a very different place than it is today. All of the matter in the universe was packed much more closely together than it is today and everything was a great deal hotter; the individual particles that make up the universe had much more energy than they have today.

Sheldon H. Glashow (left), Steven Weinberg (right), and Abdus Salam won the 1979 Nobel Prize in physics for their work on the theory of the electroweak interaction.

Glashow, Weinberg, and Salam hypothesized that the weak interaction was carried by bosons called the W and Z particles, and that when they become very hot—that is, very energetic—these particles bear a striking resemblance to the photons that carried the electromagnetic interaction. Under the energetic conditions that existed right after the birth of the universe, the two types of particles would have been completely interchangeable. And, because these were the particles that carried the weak and electromagnetic interactions, the interactions themselves would also have been interchangeable. The weak and electromagnetic interactions would have been the same. Because conditions have changed since the birth of the universe, the interactions now look different, but they are actually the same underneath.

This greatly simplified the task of explaining the weak interaction, since it now could be explained by the same theory that explained the electromagnetic interaction, or rather, by an extension of that theory. They called this new, combined interaction the electroweak interaction and concocted an electroweak theory to explain it. In 1979, they won the Nobel Prize for their efforts.

When physicists explain more than one interaction with a single theory, that theory is called a unified field theory. The unified field theory developed by Glashow, Weinberg, and Salam was not the first such theory in the history of physics. In the nineteenth century, Scottish physicist James Clerk Maxwell had shown that electricity and magnetism, previously thought to be separate phenomena, were both part of the electromagnetic interaction. In the second quarter of the twentieth century, Albert Einstein doggedly searched for a unified field theory that would show the electromagnetic and gravitational interactions to be two aspects of a single interaction, but he failed to find such a theory.

Unified field theories are an example of the kind of simplification that we have talked about in earlier chapters. By showing that the electromagnetic and weak interactions were two aspects of a single underlying interaction, Glashow, Weinberg, and Salam had reduced the number of interactions that physicists had to deal with from four to three, just as earlier generations of physicists had reduced the number of particles. This simplified the universe as studied by physicists.

Grand Unified Theories

Once it was shown that two of the four known interactions could be partially unified, physicists began looking for ways to incorporate the other two interactions into a unified theory. If the electromagnetic and weak interactions could be manifestations of a single interaction, wasn't it possible that all four known interactions could be manifestations of a single superinteraction?

Since a quantum description of the strong interaction—QCD— was already available, it was natural that physicists would next try to unify the strong interaction with electroweak theory. To some extent, they have succeeded.

Theories that attempt to unite all three of these quantum interactions—electromagnetism, weak interaction, and strong interaction—into a single interaction are called grand unified theories, or GUTs for short. Several different GUTs have been worked out to date, with many features in common. All of these theories, for instance, work on the assumption that, as the temperature rises (that is, as particles gain more and more energy) the particles that carry the forces of nature begin to look more and more alike.

And what about gravity? Is it possible to unite gravity with these other interactions? Probably it is, but no general agreement has yet been reached on how it is to be done. Theories with names such as supergravity have been worked out to explain how gravity is unified with the other interactions, but these theories have not been fully accepted by the scientific community. Most of them predict the existence of a large number of particles that nobody has yet seen in the laboratory—particles that resemble known particles yet are different, with names like electrinos, shleptons, and winos. When, and if, these particles are seen in particle accelerators, these theories may be accepted as valid explanations of the way in which the universe works. Until then, they remain speculative.

The problem with most of these theories is that they don't explain enough. They don't explain why the quantum numbers associated with elementary particles have the particular values they do, or why the interactions have the particular strengths that they do. These numbers must be plugged in "by hand" by the physicist devising the theory. If different numbers were used, the theories would still work, and this makes theoretical physicists very uncomfortable.

Another problem is that these theories still contain a number of infinities—and they are not renormalizable the way that QED and QCD are. Every time gravity enters a unified field theory, renormalizability seems to go out the window.

Further, a quantum description of gravity is still proving difficult to devise. And, until such a quantum description of gravity exists, it will be difficult to unify it with the other three interactions.

This makes the current state of particle physics seem very muddled indeed, and yet, that is not necessarily so. In 1984 a new theory (which really wasn't new at all) took the world of physics by storm. It is called Superstring Theory, and it does things that no theory has done before. It explains why certain quantum numbers have the value they do; it provides a quantum description of gravity, and offers the hope that gravity can be unified with the other three interactions; and it contains no infinities, and therefore, does not need to be renormalized. Most spectacularly of all, it reduces the number of particles that make up the universe to the smallest possible number: one.

These features mean that Superstring Theory may well be the "Theory of Everything" for which physicists have been searching for centuries.

5
Superstrings

Early in the twentieth century, physicists regarded elementary particles as tiny spheres, or balls, with measurable dimensions. This introduced problems in their theories, so they eventually abandoned this idea and came to regard elementary particles as dimensionless points, as we saw in the last chapter. This, in turn, introduced the problem of the infinities, which was solved with renormalization. And that is how things stood as of the late 1960s.

String Theory
Then, in the late 1960s, the Italian physicist Gabriele Veneziano had an idea. What, he wondered, if the elementary particles that physicists call hadrons were not tiny points at all, but tiny strings? Instead of having three dimensions (like a sphere) or no dimensions (like a point), these strings would have only a single dimension: length. They would be infinitely thin, but finitely long, about a billionth of a billionth of an inch in length.

As Veneziano and other physicists, including the American

physicist Yoichiro Nambu, worked out the ramifications of this assumption over the next several years, they realized that these strings could vibrate (like the strings of a violin or guitar), and rotate (like a spinning top). When they calculated how such a vibrating, rotating string would look to a physicist studying it in a particle accelerator, they discovered that it would look just like a hadron—and the specific way in which the string was vibrating would determine which hadron it looked like. One type of vibration would make the string look like a proton, another type would make it look like a neutron, and so forth. In a sense, the hadrons were like different musical notes produced by vibrating strings.

But we have already said that hadrons are made of quarks. How do quarks fit into string theory? According to Nambu and his colleagues, quarks are attached to the ends of the strings. (At this point, they were considering some of the strings to be Y- shaped with three distinct ends, which explains how some hadrons could be made of three quarks.)

When two strings interact with one another, they interact via their

Yoichiro Nambu, an early string theory researcher.

ends. When two strings come into physical contact, they join together at their ends to form a single string. If two strings can join together at their ends, is it also possible for a single string to join its ends together and become a kind of quantum loop? Indeed, it is. And when it was calculated what such a closed loop would look like to a particle physicist, it was discovered that it would look like a graviton, the hypothetical particle that carries the gravitational interaction.

Amazingly, string theory had spontaneously generated a quantum theory of gravity almost by accident. This was the first sign that string theory might indeed be the "Theory of Everything" that physicists were seeking.

Flaws in the Theory

Alas, there were more than a few holes in the theory. For one thing, it required a space of twenty-six dimensions in which to work.

Twenty-six dimensions? Is such a thing possible? Normal space—the kind we move about in every day—has three dimensions, which we refer to as length, width, and depth. These are simply the directions in which we have freedom of movement. Starting with Einstein's Special Theory of Relativity, physicists have also regarded time as a fourth dimension, but one in which we lack the freedom of movement that we enjoy in the other three. Thus, it has become traditional to say that we live in a four-dimensional space-time continuum.

Mathematicians have long enjoyed playing with the idea that space-time contains more than four dimensions, but only occasionally has it been suggested that such a thing might be true in non-mathematical reality. Yet this early version of string theory suggested—or, rather, demanded—that space had twenty-six dimensions. If a greater or lesser number of dimensions was assumed, the mathematics behind the theory just didn't work.

In addition, the hadrons produced by these strings weren't exactly like the hadrons that physicists observed in the laboratory. In some ways, they bore a suspicious resemblance to bosons. But some hadrons were fermions—particles of matter—rather than the more ethereal bosons. Something was obviously wrong with the theory.

By the mid-1970s, interest in string theory had waned. The problems with the theory were too great and most physicists had abandoned strings in favor of more promising theories.

Superstrings

Two physicists, John Schwarz of the California Institute of Technology and Michael Green of Oxford University, believed that string theory could be made to work. With very little support from the rest of the scientific community, they hammered away at string theory for several years, working out the problems and getting the theory into shape. In 1984, they emerged triumphantly from their studies.

The theory devised by Schwarz and Green was called Superstring Theory because it possessed a property that physicists refer to as supersymmetry. Superstring Theory was more than a theory of the hadrons: it was a theory of all particles, and of all interactions. It was the ultimate in unified field theories, a genuine Theory of Everything.

According to Schwarz and Green, all elementary particles were tiny strings, not just the hadrons. But these strings were much smaller than those envisioned earlier, about a millionth of a billionth of a billionth of a billionth of an inch in length. They were so small that in even the most powerful existing particle accelerators they would look like point particles—and yet they were not.

In effect, Schwarz and Green were saying that there was only one type of particle in the universe: the string. The type of particle that a given string appears to be depends on how it is vibrating and how it is rotating.

And what about the twenty-six dimensions of the earlier string theory? According to Superstring Theory, the universe is not twenty-six dimensional but ten-dimensional. And where did the additional six dimensions come from? Why were we not previously aware of them? Because, Superstring Theory tells us, they are very small—as small

John H. Schwarz.

as the superstrings themselves. And because they are very small, our freedom of movement in these dimensions is severely constricted. But superstrings, being as small as these miniature dimensions, have considerably greater freedom of movement within them. Physicists refer to this "shrinking" of the extra dimensions as compactification. It is not yet understood why these extra dimensions are so small while the four previously known dimensions are relatively large, but one possibility is that the discrepancy goes back to the very origin of the universe.

Superstring Theory not only allows a quantum theory of gravity, it practically leaps at the chance to provide one. The gravitational interaction appears automatically in Superstring Theory, without the need to put it in "by hand." In fact, many of the numbers that scientists have to force-fit into other theories appear naturally in Superstring Theory. Superstring Theory explains quite a few things that no other theory has come close to explaining.

Once Schwarz and Green introduced their new Superstring Theory to the world, many other physicists quickly jumped on the bandwagon. One of the first was Edward Witten of Princeton, who has made many significant contributions to the theory since Schwarz and Green announced it in 1984. Indeed, Witten has become one of its most outspoken proponents.

The Proof Is In The Strings

But the theory has also found a few detractors. Sheldon Glashow, one of the developers of the electroweak theory, is extremely skeptical of the theory. Ironically, the two other developers of the electroweak theory, Steven Weinberg and Abdus Salam, are among the theory's strongest supporters.

What will it take to prove Superstring Theory? Like most scientific theories, Superstring Theory will probably never be proven in the sense that it will be unquestioningly accepted as a true depiction of the universe. There is always room for a certain healthy skepticism in the sciences, even in regard to the most well-established of theories. Nonetheless, Superstring Theory will secure a solid position in the scientific firmament if it can not only account for all that is currently known about the behavior of forces and particles, but can be used to make predictions that are subsequently borne out by experiment.

Indeed, it readily accounts for much that is already known—far more than other proposed theories, at least according to its supporters. However, there are several reasons why it cannot yet be used to make predictions that can be verified by experiment.

We saw in Chapter Two that physicists use particle accelerators as a kind of "microscope" to examine the nature of extremely tiny particles. They do this by accelerating particles to tremendous speeds, which shrinks their wave nature to the point where they can be used to probe tinier and tinier details of matter.

But superstrings are so very, very small. They are so small that no existing particle accelerator can make a particle go fast enough to tell whether a particle is or is not a string. In fact, a particle accelerator that could accelerate particles to these speeds would be so large that it could not fit on the surface of the planet earth. Thus, at present there is no way to use a particle accelerator to test the predictions made by Superstring Theory.

And, because there is no way to test these predictions, physicists such as Glashow have suggested that Superstring Theory should not be taken seriously. The only theories that are worthy of a physicist's consideration, say these skeptics, are those theories that can potentially be proven wrong. If there is no way to prove a theory wrong, then there is also no way to prove it right.

Nonetheless, Superstring Theory is not yet complete. Physicists such as Schwarz, Green, Witten and Weinberg are even now working out the details of the theory and its ramifications. As it is better understood, it will probably be found to contain predictions that can be tested with existing equipment.

One possible type of prediction that might be used to prove

The Stanford Linear Accelerator Center. In order to prove the Superstring Theory, physicists would have to build an accelerator so large it could not fit on the planet Earth.

Superstring Theory is the prediction of new types of particles. Like most other grand unified theories, superstrings suggest that there may be types of particles in the universe of which we have previously been unaware. Some of these particles may be of a type physicists refer to as shadow matter. Shadow matter is matter that interacts with other types of matter only through the gravitational interaction. Thus, shadow matter is invisible (because vision is a kind of electromagnetic interaction), but it does produce gravity. If a shadow matter planet came into the vicinity of the earth, we would not see it—but we sure would feel it!

Assuming that such a close encounter between the earth and a shadow matter planet does not occur, how can we detect such shadow matter? It won't be easy, especially over long distances, because of the weakness of the gravitational interaction. But experiments to verify the existence or non-existence of shadow matter will probably be developed sooner or later, and they might tell us a lot about the validity of Superstring Theory.

Explaining the Universe
One of the most exciting things about Superstring Theory—and about unified field theories in general—is that it can help us understand the origin of our universe. When the universe was a fraction of a second old, it was full of extremely dense matter, and it is even possible that the universe itself started out the size of a single string, a millionth of a billionth of a billionth of a billionth of an inch across. Conventional theories can tell us nothing about what such a highly compressed universe would be like because conventional theories cannot describe how matter would behave under such conditions.

Unified field theories suggest that all four known interactions would have been identical to one another at that moment, that there was only a single superinteraction or superforce that ruled the entire universe. Superstring Theory may tell us what that superinteraction was like.

And once we know what this superinteraction was like, we may be able to answer questions that have baffled scientists and philosophers for centuries, even thousands of years, questions like: Why does the universe exist? What existed before the universe? And, of course: Why is the universe the way that it is?

If Superstring Theory is validated, Stephen Hawking's suggestion that the end of theoretical physics is in sight may turn out to be correct. Superstring Theory tells us that the universe is made of only one type of particle, the string, and one type of interaction, the superinteraction. And eventually, it may tell us why everything is the way that it is. Then there will be nothing for particle physicists to do, except work out the many ramifications of the theory.

But that, in fact, is a job that may take centuries, or even thousands of years. Like the detective explaining the simple solution behind a complicated mystery, physicists may have quite a job explaining how the simple rules of our universe are translated into the undeniably complex world that we see around us every day. Stars, planets, and human beings may be constructed from something as simple as tiny strings, but that doesn't mean that stars and planets—and, especially, human beings—are themselves simple. Complexity can be made out of simplicity, and it is complexity that will keep the study of science interesting for a long time to come—even if the universe itself turns out to be the simplest place imaginable.

Glossary

aces—An early name for the particles that eventually became known as quarks.

anti-matter—Matter made up of the anti-particles (with reverse charges) of the particles that make up ordinary matter.

anti-quarks—The anti-particles of quarks.

asymptotic freedom—The way in which the force between quarks grows stronger with distance.

atomic theory—The theory, once controversial but now accepted, that all matter is made of particles called atoms.

atoms—The particles, once thought indivisible, that make up all ordinary matter.

bosons—Subatomic particles that obey the rules devised by the physicist Satyendra Bose.

compactification—The reduced size of several dimensions of space postulated by modern unified theories, compared to the size of the familiar three dimensions.

compounds—Materials made up of a combination of elemental substances (elements).

cosmic rays—Subatomic particles traveling through space at high speeds, which occasionally enter the earth's atmosphere.

cosmic ray shower—A cascade of subatomic particles that occurs when a cosmic ray collides with a particle of the earth's atmosphere and its energy is converted into new particles, which collide with other particles creating still more particles, and so forth.

electric charge—A property of subatomic particles that governs the electromagnetic interaction between those particles; it can be either "positive" or "negative."

electromagnetic interaction—The interaction that occurs between electrically charged particles. Particles with like charges repel one another and particles with opposite charges attract one another.

electron microscope—A microscope that views objects by bouncing electrons off of them.

electron neutrino—A fundamental particle.

electrons—A fundamental particle and one of the building blocks of the atom.

electroweak theory—The Nobel Prize-winning scientific theory that explained both the electromagnetic and weak interactions as aspects of a single interaction, called the electroweak interaction.

elements—The fundamental materials that make up ordinary matter, the nature of the element determined by the number of protons in its atoms.

experimental scientists—Scientists who gather data about the universe by performing experiments and recording the results; as opposed to theoretical scientists.

fermions—Subatomic particles that obey the rules devised by the physicist Enrico Fermi.

gluons—The particles that carry the color interaction between quarks.

grand unified theories (GUTs)—Theories that attempt to explain all four fundamental forces as aspects of a single force.

gravitational interaction—An interaction that occurs between all particles with mass, producing a mutual attraction between the particles.

graviton—The particle that carries the gravitational interaction between particles with mass.

hadrons—Particles that are made up of combinations of three quarks; the only particles that undergo the strong interaction.

interactions—The ways in which particles affect other particles, by attracting them, repelling them, or changing their quantum numbers; there are four fundamental interactions, the gravitational, electromagnetic, weak and strong interactions.

inverse square principle—The way in which certain forces between particles fall off with distance.

leptons—A group of six fundamental particles consisting of the electron, electron neutrino, muon, muon neutrino, tau particle and tau neutrino.

mass—A property of subatomic particles that determines the gravitational interaction between them.

mesons—Particles originally theorized as the carriers of the strong force between hadrons.

metaphor—A symbolic manner of expressing a concept, such as the description of gravity as curved space (though this particular description is also scientifically useful).

microscope—A device for studying very small objects.

muon—A subatomic particle unexpectedly discovered in the 1940s, leading to the further discovery of dozens of hadrons (a proliferation of particles eventually explained by quark theory).

neutrons—Subatomic particles that are one of the building blocks of the atom (and that are in turn made up of quarks).

nucleus—The central body of the atom, made up of protons and neutrons held together by the strong force.

Occam's Razor—A scientific rule of thumb that suggests that the simplest theory that explains all known facts is usually the best.

particle accelerators—Machines used to propel subatomic particles to high speeds and then collide them with other particles in order to examine the submicroscopic structure of those particles.

particle physics—The study of the fundamental particles that make up all matter and the interactions that occur between them.

photons—The particles that make up light.

physics—The study of the fundamental laws that govern the behavior of matter, space, and time.

probability waves—"Waves" made up of the changing probabilities of certain subatomic events occurring; according to the standard interpretation of quantum mechanics, everything in the universe is made up of such waves.

protons—Subatomic particles that are one of the building blocks of the atom (and that are in turn made up of quarks).

quantum chromodynamics (QCD)—The body of theory that explains the "color" interactions between quarks and the strong interactions between hadrons (which are two forms of the same interaction).

quantum electrodynamics (QED)—The body of theory that explains the electromagnetic interactions between electrically-charged particles.

quantum numbers—The set of numbers that uniquely describe each kind of subatomic particle.

quantum theory—The body of theory that explains the fundamental particles and interactions that make up the universe as the interaction of probabilities.

quarks—The fundamental particles that make up the subatomic particles called hadrons (e.g. protons and neutrons).

relativity—The body of theory that explains the gravitational interaction.

renormalization—A method of removing infinities from theories such as QED and QCD by subtracting opposing infinities from one another.

shadow matter—A theoretical type of matter that interacts with normal matter only through the gravitational interaction (and thus is invisible to our eyes and telescopes, which operate through the electromagnetic interaction).

strong interaction—The interaction by which hadrons attract one another; actually a manifestation of the more fundamental color interaction between quarks.

Superstring Theory—A body of theory that proposes that all fundamental particles are actually a single fundamental particle referred to as the "string," which can take on a number of properties and quantum numbers.

tau—A fundamental particle.

tau neutrino—A fundamental particle.

telescope—A device for magnifying images and drawing in large amounts of light from faraway objects.

theoretical scientists—Scientists who devise theories to explain the data gathered by experimental scientists.

Theory of Everything—A long-sought scientific theory that would explain everything known about the universe in a single equation or set of equations.

unified field theories—Theories that explain two or more of the four fundamental forces as aspects of a single underlying force.

weak interaction—A fundamental interaction that actually changes the quantum numbers of the interacting particles, converting them to different kinds of particles.

W particles—One of the two types of particles that carry the weak interaction between particles.

Z particles—One of the two types of particles that carry the weak interaction between particles.

Index

L
leptons, 24

M
mass, 27-29
Maxwell, James Clerk, 46
mesons, 33
messenger particles, 34
microscope, 16
muon, 24
muon neutrino, 24

N
Nambu, Yoichiru, 50
neutrons, 14-15, 21, 24, 32

O
Occam, Sir William of, 11
Occam's Razor, 11

P
particle accelerators, 21, 55
photons, 16, 25, 35
pixels, 42
point particles, 41
probability waves, 18
protons, 14-15, 21, 24, 32

Q
quantum chromodynamics (QCD), 43-44, 47
quantum electrodynamics (QED), 38-43
quantum numbers, 24
quantum theory, 15
quarks, 22-24

R
relativity, 36-38, 51
renormalization, 43

S
Salam, Abdus, 44-47, 54
Schwarz, John, 52, 54-55
scientific method, 6
shadow matter, 57
strange quarks, 23
strong interaction, 27, 29, 30, 32, 33, 43-44
superstring theory, 48, 49-58
supersymmetry, 52

T
tau neutrino, 24
tau particle, 24
theoretical scientist, 7
"Theory of Everything," 8-10, 48, 52
top quarks, 23

U
unified field theories, 9-10, 46-48
universe, origin of, 57
up quarks, 23-24

V
Veneziano, Gabriele, 49

W
waves, 18
weak interaction, 27, 29, 32-33, 44-47
Weinberg, Stephen, 44-47, 54
Witten, Edward, 54, 55
W particles, 35, 46

Y
Yukawa, Hideki, 33-34

Z
Z particles, 35, 46
Zweig, George, 22-23